WEIRD SEA CREATURES™

THE MORAY EEL

Miriam J. Gross

The Rosen Publishing Group's
PowerKids Press™
New York

For Allison and Suzanne

Published in 2006 by The Rosen Publishing Group, Inc.
29 East 21st Street, New York, NY 10010

First Edition

Editor: Daryl Heller
Book Design: Albert B. Hanner

Photo Credits: Cover, p. 5 © Stephen Frink/Corbis; p. 6 © Kit Kittle/Corbis; p. 9 © Jay Syverson/Corbis; p. 10 © Hal Beral /V&W/ SeaPics.com; p. 13 © Robert Yin/Corbis; p. 14 © Stephen Frink/Corbis; p. 17 © AEF/Tony Malquist/ Getty Images; pp. 18, 21 © Doug Perrine / SeaPics.com.

Library of Congress Cataloging-in-Publication Data

Gross, Miriam J.
  The moray eel / Miriam J. Gross.
      p. cm. — (Weird sea creatures)
  Includes index.
  ISBN 1-4042-3189-7 (library binding)
  1. Morays—Juvenile literature. I. Title. II. Series.
  QL638.M875G76 2006
  597'.43—dc22

                              2004025425

Manufactured in the United States of America

CONTENTS

MEET THE MORAY EEL

Moray eels are long fish that look like snakes. Divers often spot them in the **cracks** in **coral reefs** opening their mouths and showing a jaw full of razor-sharp teeth. Many people are afraid of moray eels because of their scary appearance. However, these shy fish will not usually try to harm people.

Scientists have separated fish into groups to study them. Eels belong to a large group known as bony fish. Scientists separate fish from large groups into smaller groups called families and species. There are 18 other families of eels besides morays. In the moray family there are more than 100 species, or different kinds, of eels.

All eels have long, smooth bodies made for digging down into the sand or slipping between rocks. Morays are bigger than most other eels and average about 5 feet (1.5 m) in length. Most other fish have scales to **protect** their skin, but moray eels do not. Morays produce **mucus**, which they **secrete** over their bodies. This mucus protects a moray's skin from **germs** and makes its body slimy.

Green moray eels, such as the one shown here, make their home near the shore. Some green moray eels have been known to keep the same home for about seven years.

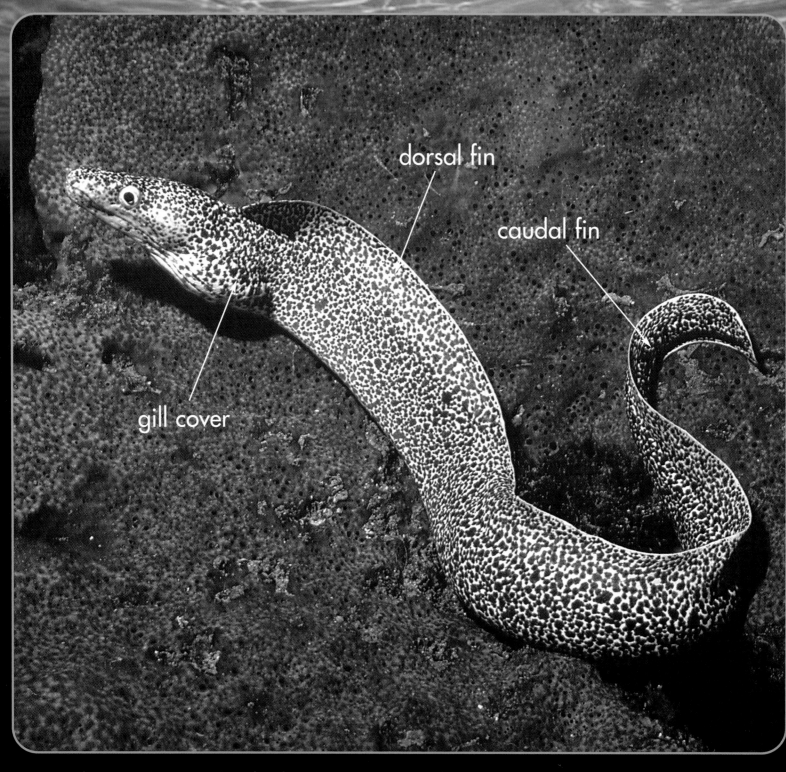

dorsal fin

caudal fin

gill cover

This spotted moray eel is often found in sea grass meadows. A sea grass meadow is an area near the shore that has grasslike plants, such as sea grass, growing in shallow, or not very deep, water. This animal likes to be alone. Care should be taken not to bother a spotted moray as its bite can be quite painful.

WIGGLING IN THE WATER

Eels are vertebrates, or animals with backbones. Their backbone has nearly 100 bones called vertebrae. The vertebrae make the eel's backbone **flexible** and allow the eel to move like a snake. Moray eels have three fins that help them swim and turn in the water. The dorsal fin runs along the eel's back. The anal fin runs along its belly, or stomach. The caudal fin is at the tail. Morays swim by moving their bodies from side to side in an S-shaped wave.

Moray eels breathe by means of gills, which are **organs** that take oxygen from water. Oxygen is a gas that is necessary for animals to breathe. As water flows through the gills, it enters the fish's bloodstream and is sent through its body. To breathe the eel draws water into its mouth and then over the gills that are inside the moray's body. Next it passes the water through its body and out small covered holes called gill slits. For the moray to take in enough oxygen, it must keep opening and shutting its mouth. What looks like a scary display of teeth is just the moray's way of breathing.

WHERE MORAY EELS LIVE

Moray eels live mainly in shallow, or not very deep, warm waters in **tropical** and **subtropical** seas all over the world. They are often seen in the Bahamas, the Caribbean, the Gulf of Mexico, and parts of Asia. Morays are sometimes found in the Atlantic coastal waters of North Carolina, South Carolina, and New Jersey.

Morays are shy creatures that usually live alone in caves or in cracks in coral reefs. Coral reefs are underwater hills that are filled with a community of colorful plants and animals.

To blend in with their surroundings, many morays have brightly colored or patterned skin. Depending on where they live, some morays have green skin. Others have zebra stripes or spots on their skin. This camouflage, or method of hiding, allows morays to surprise their **prey** and hide from **predators**. Since they keep their mouths open to breathe, the insides of their mouths are sometimes colored or patterned as well.

This brown-spotted moray eel is hiding in a crack in a coral reef. This coral reef is part of Kealakekua Bay, off the coast of the U.S. island of Hawaii.

The size of an animal affects the type of prey the animal is able to catch. Smaller moray eels dine on crabs. Larger species, or types, of morays, such as this spotted moray eel, eat fish.

A Sharp-toothed Carnivore

Moray eels are carnivores, which means they eat other animals. They have strong jaws that open wide to bite pieces of food. Most morays have sharp, pointed teeth to help them capture soft-bodied prey, such as fish and octopus. Some types of morays, such as the zebra moray in the Philippines, have dull, rounded teeth. These teeth are better for squashing the shells of **crustaceans**, such as shrimp and crabs.

Morays sometimes swallow their prey whole. After swallowing large prey, the moray curls its body into a tight knot. This breaks the bones of its prey and flattens the food. The food is then able to be digested, or broken down, more easily.

Morays usually hide in their holes during the day with only their heads poking out. If prey passes by, morays dive from their holes and grab the animal with their teeth. When night falls moray eels go out hunting. Although morays have poor eyesight, their sharp sense of smell helps them hunt in the dark.

PREDATORS

Few animals eat the moray eel other than grouper fish and other moray eels. The moray's large size and sharp teeth scare off most other predators. Their slimy bodies also make them hard to catch. In some species, such as the starry moray, the mucus that covers their bodies is also toxic, or poisonous, to other animals.

Although people catch and farm many other species of eels for food, they hardly ever eat morays. The moray's flesh often has a bad taste and may cause an illness called ciguatera fish poisoning.

Ciguatera fish poisoning gives people a stomachache that lasts for days. The poisoning can also cause weakness in the arms and legs. Cooks should be careful if they plan to serve eel for dinner, as it is hard to tell a safe eel from a poisonous one.

This starry moray does not have much to fear when it goes in search of food. The mucus that covers its body makes this creature toxic to other animals. The inside of a starry moray's mouth is yellow to match its usual ocean hideout in a coral reef.

This cleaner wrasse has tiny teeth that it uses to eat food from the body of a moray eel. When animals, such as a moray eel, swim into an area so that other fishes can clean them, this area is called a cleaning station.

Is This a Friend or an Enemy?

The wrasse is a tiny fish that spends a lot of time close to the moray eel's sharp teeth. The moray eel does not harm the wrasse, however. The wrasse helps the moray eel. The small fish eats the worms, **fungi**, and other **parasites** that stick to the eel's head, gills, gums, and lips. In this way it cleans the eel while having a meal.

This is an example of a symbiotic relationship, in which two different kinds of animals benefit from helping each other. The moray eel helps the wrasse by giving it free food and safety from other predators. The wrasse keeps the moray eel clean and healthy.

The sabretooth blenny fish looks like the wrasse. Therefore, the moray eel lets the sabretooth blenny get close. However, this fish is no helper. The sabretooth blenny takes a bite out of the moray's lip, wounding it, and then quickly swims away.

Mating Habits

The mating habits of eels bewildered scientists for centuries. They were unable to capture any eels with eggs, and they never saw any young eels in the water where the adult eels lived. Finally in 1922, a Danish scientist named Johannes Schmidt discovered that European eels spawned in the Sargasso Sea. Those same adult eels that people saw in European rivers made a journey of thousands of miles (km) to produce young. By the time the young made it back to Europe, they were already full-grown eels.

In the summer months when the water is warmest, male and female moray eels gather to **mate**. Morays open their mouths wide to show each other that they are ready to make babies. Then they wrap their bodies together for hours. Moray eels spawn, or drop their eggs, close to their homes about 328 to 656 feet (100 to 200 m) below the surface.

Large female eels can drop between 5 and 13 million eggs at a time. Males then **fertilize** the eggs, which are about the size of a pinhead. The eggs have a drop of oil that makes them lighter than water. Therefore, they float up from the deep water. A baby eel will grow inside the egg for several days before it breaks the egg open. During this time other animals will eat millions of the eggs.

When moray eels mate they stay in the same area together for a period of time. Later the two morays separate and live apart from each other.

This is a leptocephalus larva, or a baby eel in an early stage of its life. Later the larva will become thinner. When the eel matures, or gets older, it will go through a metamorphosis. This means the look of the eel will completely change. After metamorphosis the adult eel will have a different form and color.

LIFE CYCLE

The creatures that come from eel eggs are larvae. They do not look like the adults they will become. These clear, leaf-shaped larvae are called leptocephali. They have no fins and cannot swim. However, they do have tiny, sharp teeth. Through their skin you can see the heart and the notochord, which is the beginning of the vertebrae.

In this early stage, the leptocephali drift in water currents and eat **plankton**. Over the next eight months, the larvae grow and begin to look more like eels. They become rounder and grow fins, which help them swim. Later on their skin darkens, and they grow a new set of teeth. Teeth allow the eels to eat plants and small animals. A metamorphosis is what scientists call such a complete change of an animal's appearance. A metamorphosis can be a change inside an animal, too.

Once they become large enough to fight off predators, usually after eight months, the young eels make their way to shallower water. They will spend most of their lives in shallow water. Most eels live between 10 and 20 years.

A MIX OF MORAYS

The giant moray eel lives in waters from India and Sri Lanka to Australia. This creature is sometimes found in freshwater. The green moray eel can be found from the Florida Keys to Brazil and sometimes even as far north as the U.S. state of New Jersey.

The largest moray eel is the giant moray, which can reach lengths of 11.5 feet (3.5 m). The giant moray is gray-brown in color and lives in shallow waters and **lagoons**.

Green morays live in harbors, coral reefs, and underwater meadows of sea grass. Growing to lengths of up to 7.5 feet (2.3 m), these large animals are known for eating other morays. The green moray's skin is actually dark brown. The covering of yellow mucus makes it look bright green.

The dragon moray looks like it has horns growing out in front of its eyes. These are really another form of nose that improves this species' sense of smell. Dragon morays can grow up to 3 feet (91 cm) long. Their bodies are brownish orange with small spots that are black and white. Their heads have orange and white stripes.

A dragon moray eel can be found in the coral reefs off the island of Hawaii. Similar to the mouths of many other species of moray eels, the inside of a dragon eel's mouth is patterned like the rest of its body.

Moray Eels and People

Wealthy people in ancient Rome loved morays so much that they kept them as pets in ponds near their homes. One woman was said to have given her eel a pair of earrings. People believe that Romans would throw slaves who did not do what they were told into ponds filled with eels that would eat humans. Today people keep very small types of morays as pets in fish tanks.

The same coral reefs and warm, clear waters in which moray eels make their home are also favored by divers who want to study this colorful world. In some places the divers are so common that morays have grown used to them. Some moray eels will even approach the divers hoping to be fed.

Divers must be careful not to reach their hands into holes and cracks. If they do they take the chance of getting bitten by a scared eel. Moray bites can cause deep, painful wounds. **Bacteria** living in the moray's mouth can cause serious **infections**. However, if people leave morays alone these fish won't attack.

Moray eels are strange creatures that are best viewed from a distance.

GLOSSARY

bacteria (bak-TEER-ee-uh) Tiny living things that can't be seen with the eye alone. Some bacteria cause illness or rotting, but others are helpful.

coral reefs (KOR-ul REEFS) Underwater hills of coral. Coral is hard matter made up of the bones of tiny sea animals.

cracks (KRAKS) Tiny breaks or openings.

crustaceans (krus-TAY-shunz) Animals that have no backbone and have a hard shell and limbs, and that live mostly in water.

fertilize (FUR-tih-lyz) To put male cells inside an egg to make babies.

flexible (FLEK-sih-bul) Being able to move and bend in many ways.

fungi (FUN-jy) Living things that are like plants, but that don't have leaves, flowers, or green color, and that don't make their own food.

germs (JERMZ) Tiny living things that can cause sickness.

infections (in-FEK-shunz) Sicknesses caused by germs, or tiny living things that can make people sick.

lagoons (luh-GOONZ) Shallow ponds or channels near a larger body of water.

mate (MAYT) To join together to make babies.

mucus (MYOO-kus) A thick, slimy liquid produced by the bodies of many animals.

organs (OR-genz) The parts inside the body that do a job.

parasites (PAR-uh-syts) Living things that live in, on, or with another living thing doing it harm.

plankton (PLANK-ten) Plants and animals that drift with water currents.

predators (PREH-duh-terz) Animals that hunt and eat other animals.

prey (PRAY) An animal that is hunted by another animal for food.

protect (pruh-TEKT) To keep from harm.

secrete (sih-KREET) To make a liquid or gas and then let it out.

subtropical (sub-TRAH-pih-kul) Just outside the warmest parts of Earth.

tropical (TRAH-pih-kul) Having to do with the warm parts of the Earth that are near the equator, where it is warm year-round.

INDEX

WEB SITES

Due to the changing nature of Internet links, PowerKids Press has developed an online list of Web sites related to the subject of this book. This site is updated regularly. Please use this link to access the list:

www.powerkidslinks.com/wsc/morayeel/